First published in North America in 2013 by Boxer Books Limited.
First published in Great Britain in 2011 by PatrickGeorge.
www.boxerbooks.com

Text and illustrations copyright © 2011 PatrickGeorge.

Library of Congress Cataloging-in-Publication Data available.

The illustrations were prepared digitally by PatrickGeorge.
The text is set in ITC Avant Garde Gothic.

ISBN 978-1-907967-54-2

1 3 5 7 9 10 8 6 4 2

Printed in China

MAGIC
COLORS

BOXER BOOKS

brown bear

green frog

yellow candy

green bird

brown rabbit

yellow car

red train

green ball

brown ball

brown leaves

green leaves

orange sunset

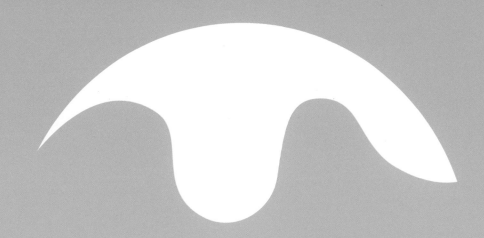

chocolate ice cream

green grapes

purple grapes

blue sky

green grass

white mouse

black cat

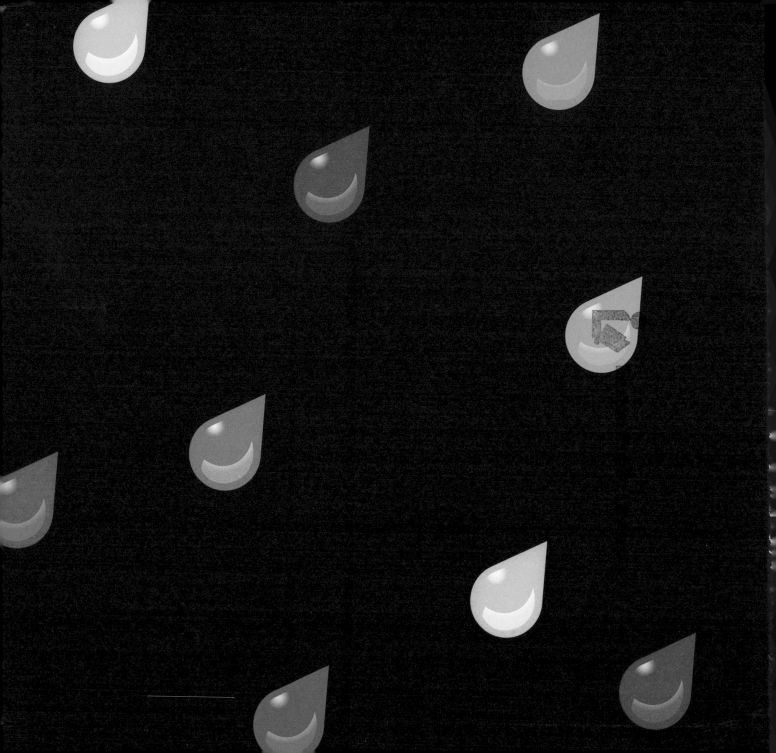